Like Ghosts

Like Ghosts

Shirley Steele

QBMM PUBLISHING
BILLINGS MONTANA

Project coordinator Julie Schultz, This House of Books

Copyeditor & proofreader Julie Schultz

Cover and book design Rosanna Buehl

Cover art *Winter on the Reservation* by Ben Steele (used by permission)

This book is typeset in the Adobe Jenson typeface family designed by Robert Slimbach from Adobe Originals.

Printed and bound in the United States of America.

ISBN: 979-8-9876996-4-5

QBMM Publishing
3544 Toboggan Road, Billings, Montana, USA
Email inquiry@qbmm.com
Tel 1-406-248-3802

Books by Shirely Steele are available in store, online, or by telephone at This House of Books. Support indie bookstores.

116 North 29th St., Ste. B, Billings, Montana, 59101-2029
Email billingsbookstore@gmail.com
Web thishouseofbooks.com
Tel 1-406-534-1133

Dedicated to the
New London Public Library, Ohio

Foreword

Shirley's first collection of poetry, *West of Town,* was wide-ranging. It covered a variety of geographies and topics, including people's daily lives, nature, and the landscape. Always pithy and insightful, this breadth has characterized Shirley's poetry over many years.

In earlier Montana days, much of Shirley's work found its way into the activities of the Billings Arts Association and the Montana Institute of the Arts (MIA). In addition to her poetry, she wrote the MIA Bookshelf in *Montana Arts.* In this section of the statewide journal, Shirley focused on publications emphasizing Montana and the West, themes in her poetry.

Shirley's poetry has appeared in varied publications over the years. Seasons and nature often figure into her poems, always with a tactile sense of things, making you feel like you are in the poem. This second collection of poems centers on nature even more prominently, highlighted with her characteristic frugality of words and sharpness of imagery.

Shirley gives you an image, often very mundane, and draws you into the profoundness that is beyond it. That's what has always stood out to me: A simple observation, nicely described—with the observer often in the background in this collection—almost compelling the reader to think about the larger meaning and mysteries behind it. This is the treat that Shirley gives us. Enjoy this collection.

—*David Darby*

Contents

Foreword *vi*

How I Hate the Wind Today 1

After Dark 2

Powder 3

Haiku 4

Poems on the Fridge 5

Stone House 6

Old Apple Trees 6

I Should Do Some Haiku 7

Warming   11

Visitor   12

Rosemarie   13

Haiku   14

Winter Bird   16

Science Says   17

Adelaide Crapsey Cinquains   18

Acknowledgements   20

About the Author   22

Also by Shirley Steele   26

How I Hate the Wind Today

The way it picks at the boards
and battens of the house
with long, strong fingers
and shakes the spruce trees along the alley.
They shrug big shoulders and
fling their cones and pieces
of old nests about the yard.

After Dark

Like an errant child
at play after dark,
the wind
rolled snowballs
on the lawn last night.

Powder

The feel of steel
slicing snow –
the wing of a plane
through a cloud.

I fly. I fly
down
down
the mountain.

Haiku

Finding a shell
not perfect –
mine.

🌀

Snow holds the hedge
in frozen captivity –
one branch sways free.

🌀

Boys in the alley
on a September evening
applefighting.

Poems on the Fridge

Moment
under rain.

You true and cool.

Summertime –
lake spirit
always with me.

Smooth power
never humble.
Temptation to rob.

Earth and heaven
are dark.
We need a holy storm.
Run now!

Stone House

Etched bird wings
and little mouse things,
dark sand from prehistoric shores,
darker ash from world beginnings,
moss from ancient forest floors and
shells of layered atom rings

lichen jeweled,
ivy draped –

these to own
in a house of stone.

Old Apple Trees

Eve's curse,
"King of fruits"
prize of Hercules
from the far-off Hesperides.
Cause, they say, of the Trojan War.
Celts in Britain dipped for them
to foretell the future.
Norseman ate them to stay
    young forever.
Old ones bear their history well
but show the scars.

I Should Do Some Haiku

A stubborn old tree
resists the turn of autumn –
the valley dozes.

❧

Eyes wide open
behind closed lids –
no sleep tonight.

❧

Spruce needles
fly in the wind –
no rain.

❧

Starlings, black
against the green lawn
drink from the birdbath.

～ઝ～

Tiny tracks in snow
tell stories of those who live
in yard and garden.

～ઝ～

Small visitors come
in the snow to the garden.
Are they hungry?

～ઝ～

Huskies love to run.
Runners cut through frozen snow –
a long way to go.

～〇～

The old bachelor
props his homestead with pine poles
against the west wind.

Warming

We were pleased at first,
the sun so warm, even when
it should have been winter.

Now we begin to wonder
about certain seasons
crowding each other.

Maybe before we have time
to think about it, we'll
have the answer for Frost.

Visitor

Early Spring morning:
Crows arrive on time.
One swoops in to announce
the arrival, strutting
along the porch railing.
Next day they are gone
west to greening fields.

Rosemarie

When you fly away,
as we all do, those
who loved you
will find you.
You will not
be alone.

Haiku

A small shore bird
prints ancient messages
in the wet sand.

～❧～

Small bundles of fur
snuggle their mothers and play
in a cold March wind.

～❧～

See our large black dog
curl into a small black ball
to stay warm inside.

～❧～

Changing my seat
at the movie
once twice thrice.

⁓

The Indian caves
silently reflect the sun –
reveal few secrets.

⁓

I hear no sound
but look around
anyway.

Winter Bird

Tiny winter bird
all shades of grey
How will you survive
this bitter winter day?
What makes you stay?

Science Says

We are a species of animal
This I know.
Visits to the zoo
can be uncomfortable
but we're also a lot like plants,
flowers and weeds.
We have our time in the sun
and then we wilt away.

Adelaide Crapsey Cinquains[1]

Who knows
what is behind
each false word they utter
as they smile and promise the world
will live.

Outside
with soft, brief sighs
like the sound of a smile
the wind dances with the pine trees
all night.

I look
and find the blue
above the sandstone rim
so deep and pure I cannot take
it in.

---

1   Adelaide Crapsey, an American poet,
developed the cinquain poetic form.

At dusk
deer cross the road,
disappearing the way they came
like ghosts.

Acknowledgements

I want to start by thanking the many people over the years who taught me, invigorated me, and encouraged me. I heard it all, and it made a difference.

My heartfelt thanks go to the team at This House of Books who supported me from idea to published book. I want to especially thank Julie Schultz, who played a pivotal role in this project, juggling multiple responsibilities and without whom this book would never have seen the light of day. Rosanna Buehl, with her elegant design and typesetting skills, brought the cover and interior of my book to life, and Mark Taylor, with his meticulous attention to detail, managed all the many behind-the-scenes aspects of publishing.

Fellow poet Tami Haaland, recipient of a 2019 Governor's Humanities award, Professor of English at Montana State University Billings, and a director of the Elk River Writing Project, has long been my inspiration.

I am honored that David Darby, former federal and state official, senior US foreign advisor, long-time member of the Billings Public Library board, and dear friend agreed to write the foreword for me.

Last on the list but foremost in my mind, I want to thank my family and friends who stood by me throughout this adventure.

—Shirley Steele, August 2025

About the Author

After 68 years on Cascade Avenue in Billings, Montana, Shirley Steele now resides at Westpark Village, a senior living community. She came into this world in 1925, in Alpena, Michigan, on Lake Huron, loving the beaches, black bears, the sound of the ice breaking up in Thunder Bay, and especially the timbre of her father's voice as he lovingly read Mother Goose nursery rhymes to her in her crib.

Moving to Ohio at six, Shirley was delighted to discover Lake Erie just twenty miles north and the New London Public Library right across the street. This library became her second home. A few poems emerged during grade school and high school, more in college, and then flowed throughout her life. After earning a diploma from New London High School, she attended Ohio Wesleyan University, graduating with departmental honors in journalism and art, disciplines that she weaves into her poetry.

Upon arrival in Billings in 1959, after sojourns around the country following her husband Ben Steele's career, she became active in the Billings Arts Association and the Montana Institute for the Arts, serving in influential leadership positions in both organizations. Shirley developed her skills and started publishing poems in anthologies and journals. Over the years, she also served on editing boards. Additionally, she traveled to small towns around the state to lead poetry workshops under the aegis of the Montana Institute for the Arts.

In 1972, Shirley received the Governor's Award for the Arts. Her first book of poetry, the 2023 *West of Town*, a compilation of poems written throughout her life, was selected as a finalist for the 2024 High Plains International Book Awards. *Like Ghosts* is her second collection. On the eve of her one hundredth birthday, Shirley remains active, not only in her poetry and the civic life of her senior community, but also in preserving and promoting her husband Ben's prolific art legacy.

Shirley Steele, August 2025

Also by Shirley Steele

West of Town, Foothills Publishing,
ISBN 978-0-951053-09-6